Choosing Healthy Sexual Boundaries: The Handbook

D1523881

First edition
© 2014 by Tommy Jones and Bobby Schauerhamer

Book Layout and Design by Bill Dobbs
www.animuse.com

Published in print format by eBookIt.com
http://www.eBookIt.com

ISBN-13: 978-1-4566-2193-3

Contents

Introduction

Acknowledgments

First, Tommy would like to thank his wife, Gail, and his son, Matt, for their loyalty and support at a time of overwhelming crisis in his life. I love you both.

Thanks, also, to the entire staff, clinical and administrative, at Project Pathfinder, Inc., (projectpathfinder.org), St. Paul, Minnesota, with special gratitude to Jannine Hebert, for fixing me when I was seriously broken, and to Warren Maas for helping to restore honor and trust to my life. The healing power of this treatment program, its staff and support people, continues to contribute immensely to the health and safety of its community.

Thanks to my great friend and colleague, Bobby Schauerhamer, whose idea 10 years ago resulted in the wonderful group on which this book is based.

Bobby would like to thank all of his family, friends and employers who supported him in what he does now, rather than judging him on the mistakes that he made in the past. Thanks to all of the men who have attended the Healthy Boundaries groups over the years and share their courage and wisdom. Lastly, and most importantly, I would like to thank Tommy Jones for being steady and consistent in his friendship even as I struggle to keep from falling.

Both Tommy and Bobby would like to thank William (Liam) Dobbs for his professional design and editing work preparing this manuscript for publication.

And, of course, thanks to the Twin Cities Men's Center (tcmc.org), Minneapolis, Minnesota, for sponsoring, supporting, and providing space for the wonderful group on which this handbook is based to live and grow.

Preface

Mission Statements

The mission of Choosing Healthy Sexual Boundaries: The Support Group is to promote healthy sexual behavior among men, encourage responsible relationships, and to improve community safety through choice and maintenance of strong, well defined boundaries.

The mission of Choosing Healthy Sexual Boundaries: The Handbook is to share the cumulative experience and wisdom of this group with a wide audience of men and women who are committed to community safety.

Intended Audience

When we started our support group, *Choosing Healthy Sexual Boundaries*, we had general ideas about our intended audience. First, we felt the need for a peer facilitated, volunteer group that men convicted of sex offenses could choose to attend voluntarily, following a treatment – aftercare regimen. That is, a mechanism that would enable and strengthen maintenance of newly acquired skills and strategies learned in treatment. It would also provide a safe, comfortable and confidential venue to discuss matters of sexuality in a nonjudgmental and supportive manner. This group, we thought, would be composed of men with child sexual abuse, indecent exposure, child pornography, and molestation convictions. Many would have received court ordered treatment through private providers, not-for-profit clinics, and some from prison programs completed while incarcerated or while engaged in civil commitment. Most would be motivated to maintain and strengthen boundaries that would preclude return to jail, prison or other forms of confinement.

Our second target included men whose sexual choices were beginning to generate negative consequences, but who had not yet crossed the criminal justice boundary. Or more likely, men who had not yet been caught and arrested for illegal boundary transgressions. In education, this would be called Early Intervention. "Early," here, would mean "before going to jail." These were men cheating on wives or partners, using prostitutes, frequenting strip clubs, watching excessive pornography —including child-pornography— and engaging in unhealthy fantasy involving children and underage teens.

The goals for this audience focused on establishing or redefining individual boundaries in ways that would allow for satisfaction of sexual needs in an appropriate, healthy and harm-free manner.

A third group emerged over a period of two to three years. These were men referred by private practitioners, treatment programs, and by probation officers. They were men with potential to benefit from participating in a support group concomitant with ongoing professional treatment.

And from our time spent working with the men in this, and similar groups, comes this handbook. So who might gain from reading it? Any man who is who is concerned about his sexual behavior, choices and boundaries, who is feeling pressure from those around him to make behavioral changes, or who is experiencing negative consequences for sexual choices that are increasing in frequency and severity might benefit. Likewise, any man completing, or who has completed, voluntary or court-ordered treatment as a convicted offender and who needs help maintaining sharply drawn boundaries and remaining vigilant might give the book a try. It won't hurt; it sure may help. Good luck!

About the Authors

Thomas Jones (Tommy) was a public school teacher for 26 years. He was addicted to alcohol for much of that time. In the fall of 2001, he was in jail... a guest of the county, you might say... serving a four-month sentence in a correctional facility. It could have been worse; it could have been longer and it could have been prison. Bad choices and poor, dysfunctional and missing boundaries cost him his freedom, friends, money, trust, respect... his teaching profession.

The reasons for his incarceration are not as important as the changes within him that those consequences generated. Those changes included his decision to quit using alcohol, to choose and maintain good, healthy boundaries, and his determination to help keep his community a safer place to live.

Tommy is currently a husband, parent, friend, community volunteer and college graduate; he is also a Vietnam Veteran. In April 2013, he and Bob Schauerhamer were recipients of the Distinguished Service Award presented by MNATSA (Minnesota Association for the Treatment of Sex Abusers.)

He lives in Minneapolis with his wife and two very special cats. This is his first book.

Bobby Schauerhamer was born and raised in Minnesota, only living in other states while engaged in college studies. He graduated from the University of Minnesota, Minneapolis, earning a B.A. with magna cum laude honors and a major in psychology in 1973. He then attended and graduated from Western Michigan University with honors earning an M.A. in experimental psychology in 1976. During the past decade he has attended several classes at the Loft Literary Center in Minneapolis where he finds valuable solace, balance in his life and the opportunity for creative expression.

He had the opportunity to work in research throughout his college education starting with surgical research at the University of Minnesota as an undergraduate. Four professional publications resulted from that research with his first article as primary author, which was published in *The American Journal of Surgery* in 1972 (1972, Schauerhamer, R., et al).

Mr. Schauerhamer was licensed as a psychologist in the State of Minnesota in 1979 and surrendered that license in 2001. He pursued a second career in the print and manufacturing industry following a brief period of recovery. He is now certified to operate several large format digital presses and has a forklift license.

Bobby has been a member and participant at the Twin Cities Men's Center (tcmc.org) in Minneapolis for over three decades. He and Tommy Jones created and began to facilitate the *Choosing Healthy Sexual Boundaries* support group at the TCMC in April of 2004. The *Choosing Healthy Sexual Boundaries* group has been meeting weekly since that time and developed sufficient interest to generate a second group, which began meeting in St. Paul in 2010. Scores of men have participated in these groups over the years. At the time of this writing there are six trained facilitators servicing these groups.

Bobby was recognized for his community service with the Ron Hering Award, granted on January 15, 2011 by the Minnesota ManKind Project. He and Tommy also received a Distinguished Service Award granted by the MNATSA in 2013 in recognition of their contributions to keeping our community safe.

What this Handbook is and is not

We are not therapists. And this is not a therapy-based handbook, just as our support groups are not therapy groups. Suggestions you find within these pages will include seeking the help of a therapist, counselor or other mental-health care professional. And while we believe that most of us need some form of professional assistance when we undertake substantive behavioral change, it will not come from this book. We will not tell you what to, how to, or when to do anything. Nor will we insist that you need to, have to, should, ought or must do anything specific in order change and improve. And neither is this a workbook. It does not include exercises, charts or graphs, assignments, data spreadsheets, list compilations, journaling requirements or personal inventories. Of course, these techniques can all be helpful and productive when used correctly and consistently. Pursue them if you find them helpful or think they could be so. A man, new to our group and after his first visit, once asked, "...well, aren't you going to tell me what to do?" "Afraid not..." was our answer. Just as we do not prescribe behavior in our groups, neither does this book.

What this handbook will do, however, is provide suggestions, choices and options for establishing healthier boundaries, and support you in your journey to achieve them. Many of these suggestions are actually tools and strategies that men have successfully incorporated into their lives. We have seen them work; they have worked for us. Is the list of tools exhaustive? Nope. Lots of room exists for each of us to add new stuff. Will you use all of them? We doubt it. You may try them all, but some will fit better than others. Some will supply you with stronger support and more lasting success. Use this handbook as a sourcebook of ideas... but do not use it as a substitute for professional care, or as your only source of guidance.

The Handbook

Why Boundaries?

"Good fences make good neighbors," Robert Frost wrote. They also make good boundaries. So do NO TRESPASSING signs. Well, maybe not good neighbors, but good boundaries, for sure. Personal boundaries are like fences and signs. They mark the edges or limits of our personal space. They help protect our identity and individuality. They separate us from others in a safe and healthy way. Our boundaries include those of personal space, our physical bodies, communications, emotions, social areas such as family, friends and work. Boundaries are important because they protect our identity, honesty, our feelings and needs, our goals, values, morals and our own well-being.

We all actually have three types of boundaries. Or maybe, boundaries that function in three different ways. Our boundaries keep us safe from others who have absent or poorly defined boundaries of their own. They can also keep others safe from us. And they hopefully keep us safe from ourselves. Many of us have violated the boundaries of others at some time, and have chosen boundaries that have not worked to protect ourselves. But we have also allowed others to cross or ignore our own boundaries in harmful ways.

What Are Safe Healthy Boundaries?

What, then, are good boundaries? What do they look like?
Healthy boundaries:

- ∞ Keep a safe physical and emotional distance between us and others.

- ∞ Allow us to say "no" without guilt.

- ∞ Define the line that if crossed has resulted in negative consequences in the past.

- ∞ Define the line that, when violated, may result in verbal, physical, emotional or sexual abuse.

- ∞ Allow others to keep a healthy emotional distance from us.

- ∞ Allow balanced physical and emotional space between us and others.

- ∞ Emphasize respect for the boundaries of others, and for our own.

What Are Unhealthy Boundaries?

These are signs of poor, soft, unhealthy or poorly defined boundaries. Do any of them sound familiar?

∞ Acting on first sexual impulse.

∞ Contradicting your own personal values or morals to obtain pleasure.

∞ Ignoring the boundaries of others.

∞ Lacking respect for the boundaries of others.

∞ Touching others without their permission.

∞ Allowing others to abuse your boundaries for any reason.

∞ Expecting someone to meet your needs automatically.

∞ Sexually, verbally or physically abusing anyone.

∞ Encouraging others to ignore their boundaries.

∞ Sharing too much too soon.

∞ Inability to say "No."

∞ Having a weak sense of your own identity.

∞ Feeling powerless and then refusing responsibility for your own life.

∞ Disempowerment.

∞ Boundaries that incorporate entitlement.

∞ Boundaries founded on aggression.

Ways to Choose Healthy Boundaries

If any of the unhealthy boundaries resemble you, you might consider choosing and then resetting new boundaries. And how might you do that?

- ∞ Identify your boundary violations. What boundaries, yours and others, are you crashing or sabotaging?

- ∞ Identify irrational, unhealthy, distorted or criminal thinking, and beliefs that allow you to ignore or violate boundaries.

- ∞ Identify healthy beliefs and thinking that will help you rebuild healthy boundaries between you and others.

- ∞ Discover or retrieve strategies to build strength into these boundaries.

- ∞ Incorporate new boundaries into your life so that they keep you and others safe.

- ∞ Define your boundaries clearly.

- ∞ Adhere to your boundaries. Self-enforce them. Continually apologizing for lapses in boundary maintenance will not work.

- ∞ Give yourself time to choose and set boundaries. Selection can be a process. Do it right.

- ∞ Eliminate boundary violations from your life.

Perhaps some of the boundaries we just discussed do not seem to be related to your sexuality or to your sexual behavior. Boundaries touch and impact most of our behavior and our choices. Inappropriate and illegal sexual choices are always boundary related. Poor or soft boundaries in one area are often markers for boundary problems in other areas, including those of sexuality. Likewise, strong, appropriate boundaries foster other good boundaries, also including those related to our sexuality. Strive to develop and enhance strong boundaries in all areas of your life.

When you do think about your boundaries, when you decide to alter, improve or reset them, think about the following boundary generalities. Keep the following in mind.

We violate and disrespect the boundaries of others when we do things we should not do, and when we fail to do those things we should do. Such as the following:

- ∞ when we take advantage of weakness, insecurity, inexperience and the trust of others.
- ∞ when we say things to others that are sarcastic, hurtful or cruel, or when we ridicule and humiliate.
- ∞ when we lie and cheat.
- ∞ when we keep secrets.
- ∞ when we abandon and reject others.
- ∞ when we manipulate, mislead and groom.
- ∞ when we ignore and trash our own morals and ethics.
- ∞ when we refuse accountability and responsibility for our own harmful behavior.
- ∞ when we act without honor.
- ∞ when we use aggression and intimidation.
- ∞ and when we victimize others.

Remember. Choose your boundaries carefully. Choose those that keep others safe from you, that will keep you safe from others, and that will keep you safe from yourself. Learn to value them. Stay true to them. Continue to strengthen them. They are your boundaries; take ownership of them and responsibility for them.

Choosing Healthy Sexual Boundaries: The Group

Much of the material written in this handbook comes directly or indirectly from our support groups, *Choosing Healthy Sexual Boundaries* (www.tcmc.org/support-groups.html). Bobby and I began these unique groups in 2004. The original group had several purposes chosen to meet needs we saw existing within the community. Although 12-step groups existed to provide support for men and women dealing with issues of sexuality (Sex Addicts Anonymous, Sexaholics Anonymous), no 12-step alternatives were available.

1. We wanted a safe, comfortable, confidential setting in which men who had completed a treatment program could meet and discuss sexuality in an open, honest and intimate manner.

2. We also wanted this setting for men who had not yet crossed the criminal justice boundary but who were beginning to experience negative consequences for sexual choices, who were beginning to experience feelings of concern, guilt, remorse, fear and shame about aspects of their own behavior, and who were looking for support in choosing new, appropriate, legal and healthy boundaries.

3. A third group, men participating in treatment concomitant with support group attendance, eventually emerged. These men sought support while traversing the some times hap-hazardous journey through treatment.

Many, but not all, of the men who attend *Choosing Healthy Sexual Boundaries* have spent time in jail, prison, or in other forms of incarceration or confinement. These men often completed all or part of a treatment program in that environment. They seek strong boundaries to help them remain free. Others may not have crossed criminal justice boundaries, or may not have been caught doing so. They are searching for safe, healthy boundaries to help avoid the loss of freedom that would result from conviction of a sexual offense.

Group structure was based on a simple check-in format with each member given time to share thoughts and feelings related to the establishment and maintenance of new boundaries. Check-in feedback and anecdotal sharing of similar challenges add to a learning experience. The groups are non-confrontational but sometimes challenging, relaxed, conversational and positive. No advice is provided; no therapy given. No sponsors are mandated, no medallions, no requirements for abstinent behavior. All one needs is a desire to change and improve through adherence to appropriate, self-chosen, healthy boundaries of behavior.

So what do we mean by "choosing healthy boundaries?" For a simple example, a man comes to an HB group. He is concerned about how frequently he visits strip clubs, how much he spends on lap dances while he is there, and especially when, not if, his wife will find out. He would like to know how his problem behavior fits with a boundary group. He wonders what his boundaries should be and how to establish them. He wants boundaries to help feel better about himself and to help maintain, or save, integrity within his relationship.

Good questions. First, the group does not choose boundaries for any member. Though we may provide some guidance, suggestion or example, choice is individual responsibility. In this example, refraining from visiting strip clubs would be a logical boundary. If that is too demanding, perhaps continued visits with no lap dancing could be a initial boundary, with abstinence from clubs as an eventual boundary. Choosing boundaries does not always mean elimination or abstinence initially, but boundaries must incorporate positive change or reduction of harm, danger or risk to qualify as "healthy."

Here's another example. A gay man comes to group. He tells us that he regularly and frequently engages in risky, unprotected sex. He feels remorse and regret about his choices, and he worries about contracting STD. Though he is reluctant to abstain from promiscuous behavior entirely, he agrees that he can become fastidious about condom use. He has identified a boundary: no unprotected sex. Simple? Yes. Easy? Maybe. Appropriate boundary? You bet.

Boundaries do not need to be complex, confusing, or complicated. They should be carefully defined and stated, clearly relate to behavior and contain realistically maintainable parameters; you must have confidence that you can live within them. This does not mean that life with new boundaries is easy. They represent the kind of change and challenge that most of us find difficult and demanding; the kind of change that can benefit from participation in a support group.

The initial group was successful, with group attendance ranging from 10-20 on a regular basis. In 2011, a second group was formed to meet availability needs of men unable to attend the original group.

Leadership and Twin Cities Men's Center Facilitator Training.

Many people want to attend support groups. A smaller number want to lead one; even fewer men have leadership skills that qualify them as potential group facilitators. Identifying, selecting, recruiting and training facilitators is a difficult, ongoing and important task. Solid leadership is crucial to support group success. We aren't talking West Point or Navy Seals here — just good, solid, responsible leadership. Good facilitators who manage and lead effectively are a critical part of what keeps members returning to group. They are not easy to find. To be considered for Healthy Boundaries facilitator training, a man must first prove to be a good support group member. This means excellent attendance for at least 3 months. A good member is an attentive and respectful listener. He uses appropriate check-in etiquette, including topic selection and maintenance, good time management and regularly provides concise, positive and helpful feedback. Garnering the respect of other members is an intangible yet observable skill, and is a key quality of a potential group leader. Movement from "self-focus" to "other-focus" occurs when a member shifts primary, dominant concentration from himself and his own personal issues, to the problems and worries of other group members. This shift does not occur with all men, and can be a strong leadership marker.

Facilitating a two-hour support group is demanding. Remaining attentive to time requirements, assuring equal check-in opportunities per member, confirming that group guidelines are understood and followed, providing guidance and support for new members, modeling exemplary group behavior, injecting humor, displaying sensitivity to the special needs of specific members, managing disruptive or difficult behavior, and, most importantly, engineering a safe, respectful and confidential setting are just some of the duties involved.

For those selected, facilitator training is provided by the Twin Cities Men's Center on an annual basis. This half-day, comprehensive training includes the topics of Group Process and Check-in, Role of the Facilitator, and Support Group Techniques. Specific instruction in such areas as Safe Environment, Participant Interaction, Behavior Modeling, Active Listening, Group Guidelines and Coping with Problem Participants are emphasized.

Training is provided by experienced TCMC staff. Working facilitators also attend training sessions to review/ hone skills, and to share technique with new facilitators. Newly trained men then work under experienced guidance for a period of time.

Leadership/ facilitator training adds credence and credibility to our support groups and helps set them apart from other peer-led groups. Although peer-facilitated and community based, our groups maintain a professional atmosphere that is conducive to a meaningful, substantive and productive group experience.

When Behavior Becomes A Problem

"Behave yourself young man," is what my mom used to say. Me, of course, being the "young man." Her implication was that my behavior had crossed one of her many boundaries and was now in need of correction or redirection. She expected me to be able to return my behavior to a place within her boundaries... that I could and should terminate unacceptable actions by "behaving myself." She believed that I could control my behavior.

So what is behavior? Wikipedia defines behavior as a range of human actions that are influenced by culture, attitudes, emotions, values, ethics, authority, rapport, persuasion, coercion or genetics. And further, that "behavior of people falls within a range, with some being common, some unusual, some acceptable and some outside acceptable limits." The acceptability of certain behavior would be, we think, judged relative to social norms and, hopefully, maintained by a variety of social controls. But not always. Not when behavior falls outside acceptable limits. Not when behavior becomes a problem.

When, then, does behavior become a problem? We define behavior as a "problem" when:

1. It results in negative consequences for you...

2. ...and for others around you.

3. These consequences increase in frequency and severity.

4. You refuse to take responsibility for trying to change your behavior.

5. It becomes a source of concern and worry to those around you.

6. Your behavior leads to involvement with the criminal justice system.

We are not talking about an irritating or bad habit here. Or a guy who snores too loudly. This is behavior that has, or may result in, significant life-altering negative consequences.

Which brings us to addiction. Since we choose to describe addiction in behavioral language, that is, how an addicted person behaves, its definition is similar to that of "problem behavior," with a few additional tweaks. If you are uncomfortable with our definition, or have formed a workable one of your own, please substitute it for ours. We think that this handbook will still be helpful to you. Our view of addiction includes all addictive sources, whether they be drugs or alcohol, or behaviors such as gambling, sex, and spending. We feel addictions share more than they differ.

Addiction, then, includes several or all of these characteristic behaviors.

∞ Your addiction results in negative consequences.

∞ These consequences can involve personal / family relationships, employment, your health, finances, the legal and / or criminal justice system, or your own sense of moral and ethical values and principles.

∞ These consequences increase in frequency and severity while your addictive behavior continues.

∞ You forsake long term sources of lasting pleasure, reward and gratification in favor of those that provide immediate but temporary satisfaction

∞ You have tried to moderate or eliminate your addiction but have failed.

Addiction is much more than a bad habit, more than compulsive behavior, more than spending too much time going to the movies. Neither are there "healthy" addictions. Excessive behavior becomes an addiction only when accompanied by serious negative consequences that turn your life to chaos. But you do retain choices and options. Choosing a healthy path is one of those choices.

25 Positives: Choosing a Healthy Path

The criminal justice system has a number of methods that purport to identify men who should continue to be imprisoned after their sentence is completed (commitment), or who are most likely to re-offend. The Hare Checklist is one. Google it and see if you are a candidate to return to jail or prison. Or to go for the first time. It can be educational or downright frightening.

So what if we look at behavior and characteristics of men who chose not to return to incarceration? The kind of behavior we encourage in boundary groups. What do those choices look like? We have gathered a list of 25 — 25 Positives, we call them. We have used all of them, and continue to do so. Many have come to us from men in boundary groups. They all work. They help keep you and your community safe. They help you keep your boundaries secure. Try them, and see for yourself. Here we go:

1. Disengage from all addictive behavior. And this really means ALL. It may take a trip or two through treatment. Sometimes more. Don't give up. Work at it until you are free. It is impossible to make consistent, healthy choices, form good boundaries and to work for positive change if you are trapped in the chaos of addiction. Find a program that matches your needs. Of course, there are many 12-step treatment programs and support groups. If you don't feel comfortable with that model, find something else. You can go on line to join a SMART RECOVERY group. There is a RATIONAL RECOVERY website. Check out Stanton Peele. VA programs are shifting to cognitive-behavioral treatment models. Find a program in which you can succeed. It's your responsibility. Oh yeah... this Positive is not optional. It is mandatory. Required. Non-negotiable.

2. Assume total ownership of your offense, the sooner the better. "Put it in your pocket", we are told in jail and treatment. You did it; you own it. It wasn't the system, and sure wasn't your victim. It wasn't your mean old dad, or your heartless, unloving mother. It wasn't something that happened to you when you were a kid. It was you; the man you see in the mirror. Take responsibility. Own it.

3. Dump the feelings of entitlement. There is very little that we "should" have or "deserve." But there is much that can be earned. Reach goals by earning trust, behaving reliably, responsibly and honestly. It will take time, and you will have to wait patiently until important others in your life decide to trust you again. And maybe some won't. Consequences for your choices will follow you the rest of your life. Most of us are worth a second chance, but none us is "entitled" to one. It's up to you to earn it.

4. Connect/Reconnect with Individuals. When we are struggling in our offender cycle, we often isolate ourselves from individuals who once played important roles in our lives: friends and relatives, teachers and clergy; coworkers, lovers and partners. Reconnecting with these people can be of critical importance in our journey to better choices and healthier boundaries. Eliminate those who helped to enable your bad behavior. Repair and nourish those relationships that are a continued positive force in your life. It will be difficult and some will reject your best efforts; most with good cause. But it is important to retrieve some, or even one. Yours is a difficult journey to complete alone.

5. Connect/ reconnect with Groups. Were you ever a group member? Church group? Hobby club? Meditation, Exercise, Reading or Writing group? No? Give one a try. Yes? Try to rejoin it or one similar. There are an unlimited number of special interest and support groups in most any urban or suburban area. They are always looking for new members... members like you. Groups allow you to form new connections, to practice your new "reliability" and "dependability" smarts, to learn new skills, talents, and interests, to make new friends. Group participation and isolation are incompatible. Groups help keep you visible and transparent. Groups can help you maintain your boundaries. Join them. Participate in them. Grow with them.

6. Connect/ reconnect with Community. You have caused your community great expense, disruption and pain. Now it's payback time. You can find lots of volunteer activities in your community: jobs that provide a real service to others. Find one that matches your skills and background. You will connect with other volunteers. Maybe make a new friend. Earn the trust of others. Your neighborhood will thank you and will appreciate your work. You will feel better about yourself. Like group work, volunteering and isolation are incompatible. Choose to be visible, open and connected. It's all good.

7. Acknowledge and accept both the existence and permanence of your darkest core demon. This one is a painful yet powerful "positive." One sunny afternoon my therapist took me on a frightening and dark journey to visit an ugly, dangerous presence in my deepest core. Well, it was actually me, but a version and vision I had never admitted to myself. I had spent much of my post-offense life denying this part of me. Oh, I would take full responsibility for my offense, but I was full of clever and self-protective quotes such as, "Yes, but I never touched anyone." "No one was really harmed," I would say. My favorite, of course, "I could never really hurt anyone." But I realized that day that the potential for such behavior was, indeed, present. And my therapist helped me to accept a troubling truth: I could see myself harming another just for the purpose of my own self-pleasure.

Doesn't sound like much of a positive? Perhaps "a necessity" would be a better descriptor. But this is a positive because it allows us to admit harsh reality about ourselves, yet to begin accepting that truth and moving on in an empowering way to...

8. ...Cage your demon in a place of impenetrable security and safety. Our responsibility does not end with identifying and acknowledging the nasty core beast. Admitting it is part of you, yet learning to feel ok or even good about yourself, requires us to keep it in a safe place. It is powerful. It will want to re-emerge; to re-establish control. It is convincing, clever, tenacious and demanding... self-absorbed and selfish. It can kill you. We must be stronger and smarter than it is. Own it but contain it.

So. Recognize your dark companion. Retain it in maximum lock-up. Stay vigilant. Keep yourself, me, our community, safe. This allows us to...

9. ...Accept our own, unconditional, inherent value and worth as a person. At certain points in our journey to find healthy boundaries, often during early stages, we find that for many reasons, people, friends and family, have decided that we are pretty worthless. We have destroyed our own "worthiness." We feel that we have little value. No one trusts us. Sound familiar? How do we recapture this sense of value? Of self-worth? Well, when it comes from no one else, then it must come from within ourselves. We have to learn to identify it when no one else will.

So how do we do this? Many clever people have written a great deal about self-worth/value, and about how to obtain and keep it. Here are a few examples.

From Smart Recovery's PRINCIPLE OF UNCONDITIONAL ACCEPTANCE (USA):
"Accept yourself just because you are alive and have the capacity to enjoy your existence. After all, you are not your past behavior. It is not your essence. And your approval of yourself does not come from others; it can only come from you. You are free to choose it at anytime."

From Vincent Fox:
"If you choose to base your worth on positive or negative comments from others, remember that these are judgments made by people who have no right to act as your self appointed judge. If you determine your worth by such judgments, your life will be miserable. Your own worth is intrinsic to you as a person, unique among all other persons. Accept and treasure it."

And from Albert Ellis:

"People should learn to truly accept themselves unconditionally, whether their therapist, or anyone else, loves them."

Funny guy, that Albert Ellis.

So find a way to discover and rediscover good things about yourself. They are there. Then believe in them. If you do, others will too... if you don't, neither will they.

10. Practice substituting remorse, regret, guilt, sadness or sorrow for SHAME. There is no upside to shame. Nothing good or positive comes from it. Ever. Oh, you may want to stick your toe into it briefly, just for the experience. Maybe to feel the sting and burn. But don't stay long, never dwell, and exit quickly. The other feelings can be healthy. They may even help you to feel responsible for your behavior and the harm it caused. It is fine, and even necessary, to feel bad about things you have done. But do not decide that you, in fact, are bad. That is the stuff of shame. You are not your deeds and they are not your essence. There is no road back from shame. Detour that one.

11. Direct / express your anger in safe, healthy ways.
Anger is a part of us all, and we all learn to deal with it in different ways. It can be a problem for us and can prevent us from staying within our chosen boundaries. Red flags for anger problems include:

- ∞   Your anger seems out of control.
- ∞   It causes you to do things you regret .
- ∞   It hurts those around you.
- ∞   You have tried to modify it in the past, and failed.
- ∞   You have used anger to threaten, intimidate or control others.

There are lots of good anger management programs around. You may have been court ordered to attend one. Do it.

Programs can be group or family-based. Ask friends for recommendations. Or ask a therapist, medical person, your probation/parole officer or someone in your support group.

12. Complete sex offender treatment, if it has been recommended or court ordered. Treatment works and can help you make real, permanent changes in your life. Put your best effort into it.

If you are not in trouble yet, but are feeling uncomfortable with your thoughts or fantasies, or are considering acting on urges or feelings that you know are wrong, inappropriate or illegal, seek professional intervention or evaluation. This is a far better choice than allowing the Criminal Justice system to make these choices for you. Don't wait. Do it today.

13. Lose the Victim Mentality. What is this you might ask? See if any of these fit you:

- ∞ You blame others for problems you have caused.
- ∞ You are unwilling to take responsibility for your own actions.
- ∞ You ascribe non-existent intentions and motives to others.
- ∞ You garner pleasure from feeling sorry for yourself. You will even beg sympathy from others by lying or exaggerating your circumstances.
- ∞ You are self-absorbed, displaying little or no empathy.
- ∞ You are defensive and create unnecessary conflict.
- ∞ You reject constructive suggestions.

None of these is good. None is conducive to choosing good boundaries, nor with living within them. There are ways to break out of this state. You may need some professional help. Google VICTIM MENTALITY for ideas and suggestions about things you can do to help yourself. Do not stay here. If you are doing any of these regularly, find a way to stop.

14. Minimize reliance on immediate gratification; establish long term, lasting sources of healthy, safe, reward and satisfaction. Those of us who have survived the chaotic life of addiction, know well the allure of immediate satisfaction and the sudden rush of excitement, whether the source be drugs or alcohol, pornography or high stakes gambling. Living within healthy boundaries, however, demands that we learn to shift to long-term sources of pleasure, satisfaction and reinforcement, and to choose rewards that are safe for us and for our community. This ability to delay gratification is one of our positives because it helps us to resist immediate temptations and urges, and to wait for later and sometimes larger reward. This tool helps us hone and strengthen personal skills like patience, self-control and will power, and helps us stay "cool and controlled" when faced with tempting "hot" situations that would take us outside our healthy boundaries. Learn to do it or find someone to help you learn.

15. Select a trusted and dependable "go to" person in case of crisis. Chose a reliable friend, sponsor, relative or partner. Some one you know well. Some one who knows you well. A person you have confided in who knows your story and who has met your beast. A person you can easily and quickly contact in case of a crisis situation. Make this person part of a safety plan. Make sure he knows your chosen boundaries. Don't wait for red flags to appear before you start searching your iPhone contacts. Have a name at the top of your list, and use it. This is a simple and easy Positive. One that can save you.

16. Seek, establish or renew at least one strong, mutual friendship. Similar to 15, but different. It may even be the same person. This could be your partner, a buddy from your past, some one from your therapy or support group, or a guy you met in jail. Yep, that can work too. If it is some one who has shared a similar struggle, speaks the language, has chosen like-boundaries or possesses a familiar beast, so much the better. We all need at least one person who truly cares about us and wants us to succeed, in order to finish our journey and stay within our boundaries. No one can really do this alone. Find, make and nurture a good friend.

17. Exercise... then exercise some more. While you are at it, begin to practice better nutrition. Lose a few pounds. Get stronger. Build up some endurance. And then...

18. Go to the doctor. Or vice versa. Get the medical checkup you have been procrastinating about ...maybe for years? Good liver function returns after you quit drinking and drugging. High blood pressure and cholesterol can be treated; extra pounds shed. Colonoscopies are not that bad. Well, they are pretty bad, but they can help prolong your life. And while you are at it, visit your friendly neighborhood dentist. Clean teeth make you feel better, not to mention make you easier to be around. Up close and personal, if you know what I mean. Hate to go to the dentist? Too bad. Go anyway. No one said Positives are all easy or fun. Good physical, mental and dental health are inseparable. They are also incompatible with poor boundaries. When you feel better, stronger and healthier, it becomes easier to maintain your boundaries. Your boundaries share your health and strength. These are some sweet Positives. Use them.

19. Become, and remain, visible, accountable and honest. When we behave addictively or with poorly defined boundaries, we tend to rely on secrets, lying, and our own forms of invisibility cloaking to help enable our choices. Lying and secrets help keep our acts private, clandestine; secluded, solitary and closeted. Invisibility keeps us unobserved, covert and deceitful. These conspire to help us circumvent negative consequences, allowing us to minimize our own feelings of remorse, guilt, shame and responsibility. We can then present an illusion of appropriate behavior while we continue to cheat and deceive ourselves and those close to us.

Learn to counter isolation and secrets by establishing visibility, dependability and reliability. Make and keep promises. Be where you are supposed to be when you are supposed to be there. Be on time. Do what you say you will and let people see you doing it. Value your own accountability. Make sure people know where you are. Use your cell to text and voicemail. People will begin to trust you. Isolation and secrets contradict good boundaries. They will pollute your attempts to change and improve. Extinguish them for good.

20. Learn, recapture, explore... a cool, safe, healthy hobby or recreational activity. "Hey, Tommy, I'm going to start playing my guitar again... Hey, Bobby, I discovered I still love doing Oil Paint-by-Numbers... Hey Tommy, I rode my bike 5 miles yesterday." We hear this all the time. And I really mean All THE TIME. It is one of the most spontaneous of all the Positives. Hobbies and healthy recreation have so many upsides. They provide opportunities to learn new stuff, to feel a sense of accomplishment and success, to polish our own self-image. Perhaps most importantly, they provide healthy distraction from potentially boundary busting urges and temptations such as the bottle of Vodka calling to you or that Website you have not visited in years. Heck, hobbies are even fun. Get one. Get two.

21. Choose your names carefully. And chose them yourself. This positive sounds a bit goofy. It is not. Don't we all have names given to us by our parents at or near our time of birth? We don't really choose our name.... or do we? Ever been to a support group that expects you to label or name yourself? Often something negative or offensive? Maybe "alcoholic," for instance. Perhaps "sex addict?" Worse yet, "pedophile?" If in prison, "cho mo" may have been sewn on your gray tee-shirt in red letters. Predator, pervert, perv; drunk, pot head, dope fiend. Lots of names. Lots of negativity. Have you incorporated any of them into your own self-identity? Your own self-image? Do they comprise a set of filters through which you view yourself? If so, not good.

Those of us dealing with the many challenges of addiction and flimsy boundaries already suffer from poor self-esteem and self-respect. Calling ourselves derogatory names in no way helps us. Actually, it helps no one, however they might view themselves. Nor is it any more "honest" to do so than referring to yourself in positive ways that foster self-respect. If we do not respect ourselves, no one else will. You are a valuable and important person first. Refer to yourself as such. What you choose to call yourself, how you think about and see yourself are factors that help determine how you feel. Choose your names carefully. Do not allow others to choose them for you. Reject labels you find personally disrespectful.

22. Remain vigilant. Remember that once you have been addicted, or have lived outside good boundaries, it is easier for you to go back down that road than it is to travel it for the first time. No matter how successful and complete you feel your changes and new boundaries have become, maintain a strong sense of vigilance and caution. Your dark passenger can and will appear at the most inopportune of times. Like when you are in a place of maximum vulnerability. "Be prepared," we called it in Boy Scouts... "situational awareness" in Vietnam. Maintain it at all times.

23. Identify and eliminate undesirable, destructive, negative, enabling personal relationships and influences. Get rid of old so-called friends and acquaintances who do not help us. We all had them. We all know just who they were. Sever those ties and populate your new life with healthy, positive friends and relationships.

24. Fine tune communication skills. Or is a major tune-up due? Whether you are renewing an old friendship, developing or maintaining a new one, looking for and then keeping a job, your communication skills play a critical role. Limited, ineffective or even non-existent skills probably contributed to your poor boundaries and risky behavior in the past. Maladaptive skills may have been part of your old offense cycle. Good, effective skills require you to communicate thoughts, feelings and needs to those around you as we'll as to understand those of others. Communication is both verbal and non-verbal. These skills can comprise a powerful positive in your life. Find ways to gain and polish these skills. Make them an important part of your life. Use them every day.

25. Find one place where you can be true to yourself; a safe setting in which you can openly share your darkness without fear or judgment, condemnation or reprisal. This place may be difficult to find. It could be a very special support group or perhaps an informal meeting of men with similar past experiences. A church group. A breakfast meeting of close friends. Try to find one. A place to talk and share in complete confidentiality and deep intimacy and trust can be a wonderful and healing positive in your life. You could even start your own group. That's what Bobby and I did. It works.

So. There you have our list of 25 Positives. You could find more, I'm certain. Empathy, self-efficacy, empowerment, and employment come to mind. Make your own list. Keep adding to it. And use it every day.

Tool Chest

There is a new task at hand for many of us. We may or may not have collected the right tools to deal with this new task. Some of the old tools just don't work so well for what we need to do, or we simply find that we are in need of some new tools. Each of us has one, and each could add to our toolkit and what we have on hand, or where we may learn more about establishing **healthy sexual boundaries**.

This section is intended to provide practical approaches to those who are interested in staying safe in the community. Staying safe here refers to being able to live in the community without engaging in sexually offensive behavior. Having the will to stay safe in the community may for some of mean that our chances of being allowed to remain in the community will be improved. This will likely involves changing some behavior, patterns, routines or habits. Changing behavior is generally not easy, but can be accomplished with the proper tools.

If you already have some favorite tools for changing your behavior and they work for you, then we support you in using those tools to accomplish those changes necessary for you to stay safe. You are likely the best judge of what works and does not work for you.

However, if you find yourself wanting more tools for changing your behavior, then this section could be helpful to you. The tools discussed within this section are just some possibilities. It is not an exhaustive list. Some of these tools may work well for some and not for others. You won't know what works until you try them.

Sometimes it may just a matter of finding the right tool. You know that you had it at one point, but now you just can't seem to find it in the toolbox. Maybe you misplaced it and did not get it back into the box, or maybe a friend borrowed it and did not return it. Let's take a look.

It is not our intention here to promote or dispute any theoretical approach to behavior change. We have no hypotheses to prove here. We only have some suggestions for some practical ways in which you might accomplish a desired behavior change.

As we look at some behavior change approaches, we will refer to those approaches as "tools." This analogy will be continued as we talk about physically storing our tools for behavior change in a toolbox or kit.

Now, as we begin working on new tasks, our toolkit may be small, containing only a few tools. Hopefully, we have become familiar with the tools that we have and how to best use them. But what if we have a novel or new task. We might not have the right tool. Even if we had the right tool, we may not have the experience in how to best use it.

This is often the way it is for men who have been confronted about their sexual behavior and demands are placed on them to change their behavior. They may feel that they don't have the right tools or the knowledge about how to use them.

The use of a new tool may take some time in order to gain proficiency. We recommend that you practice new tools for before using them in challenging situations. Try some of these tools out when the risks are not so great and when you can gain some positive experience in using them. It is helpful to know what you can expect from a tool before using it at a critical moment.

MODELING. This tool is nothing new, but applying it to a novel situation of learning how to establish healthy sexual boundaries and to be safe in the community is new. We can learn much by watching others, especially those who are successful. You can learn from other men in a sex offender treatment program by listening to what has worked for them. This may happen within a group setting where tools and strategies can be discussed in greater detail.

Many people who are attempting to change their behavior find that it is valuable to change some of their circle of friends, or if you have few friends to begin with, to find a circle of friends who can have a positive influence on you via their model of appropriate behavior and boundaries. So, for example, if your old circle of friends when you offended tend to frequent strip clubs, then it is time to change your circle of friends if you are serious about making some positive changes. Simply spending more time with men who are positive models of healthy boundaries is of value. Where you find positive models for establishing healthy boundaries is a personal choice. Just make sure boundaries are your own and meet your personal needs.

Another valuable application of this approach is to spend time one-on-one with someone who has a longer history than you of managing their own behavior to stay safe in the community. Many sex offender treatment programs require that you establish some type of relationship with a man who has greater time and experience within that program. It may be a man who has graduated from that program; or minimally a man who has shown greater progress in addressing his own safety issues in a successful way.

Some sex offender programs and certain support groups for sexual issues refer to this type of relationship as "sponsorship." Men entering and beginning a sex offender treatment program may be assigned to locate a sponsor that meets with the approval of their therapist. In some cases, the sponsor may be someone who is merely knowledgeable of the person's offense and who is willing to be in a supportive role with that man who is participating in the treatment program or support group.

Our preference is to dispense with the use of the term "sponsor" in this situation and instead to use the term **mentor** (defined here as an experienced and trusted advisor). It is our hope and your gain to find someone who is more experienced than you in accomplishing positive behavior change while being someone whom you can trust.

Establishing a relationship with a mentor can be of tremendous assistance to you in accomplishing safe management of your sexual behavior. Most time spent with a mentor can be helpful to you, especially if you are new to the experience of being held accountable for your sexual behavior. It is important here to recognize that this time is not about how much you enjoy spending time with your mentor. Don't expect that you and your mentor are always going to agree on what is the best music or where you would like to go for lunch. It is all about staying safe.

A good place to start may be just talking about it with your mentor or in a group. Listen to what others have said works for them. Talk about how you might apply it to your particular situation in the event that you might encounter a challenging event in the community.

An example might be helpful at this point. Let's say that you have an issue with being sexually attracted to certain children (the details don't matter here, just the source of the attraction). So, one man (let's call him Jim for the sake of this example) checks in at group with an experience that he shares about going into a fast food restaurant and being surprised with the presence of a group of children who are in the age range of his inappropriate interests. Jim explains that he experienced unwanted sexual excitement, and then the important part, what he did about it. Listen carefully to what he says that he did about it to stay safe, and to the feedback that he gets from other group members.

Jim related that he had a plan already worked out for what he would do when this happens. He followed his plan and immediately left the fast food restaurant, drove away, called his mentor, and eventually went to the drive through window at another fast food restaurant. Jim states a number of details including that his mentor did not answer and so he left a voice mail. He gives a lot of additional information about how he felt a little reassured when he heard his mentor's recorded voice on his message, and that he almost hit a dog driving to the second restaurant. Much of these details are simply unimportant and may just be another way for Jim to say that it was hard for him to do something different. Behavior change does not come easy.

What is important here is that Jim had a plan to stay safe. He had previously discussed it with his mentor and practiced the sequence verbally in his group. He successfully used the plan when he felt that his safety was challenged.

You will be asked to create your own safety plans if you have not already been asked to do so. It is a first step in safety and one where you can receive feedback and suggestions before you actually implement it.

Next you may be able to try out your plan in the presence of your mentor or another person whom you trust to assist and guide you if necessary. Do this when, and only when, you and your support person (mentor or otherwise) feel abundantly safe with your behavior in the community. Continue to experience successes in applying something that you have learned from a positive model and eventually it will become more familiar.

The more positive practice that we have in trying out a new safety routine, the less effort that it will seem to take. We may say that a behavior or routine is stronger or more automatic when we have had many instances of positive practice. For example, someone might say that they were so tired after work that their car drove itself home. Well, this is not true, but it probably is such a well practiced routine that it requires less effort or thought and can be done even when tired (note that driving while really tired is not being recommended here).

It is also important here to recognize that we all need some rewards for positive behavior change. Try to avoid indulging in any shame or guilt reactions related to the community safety. It would be a mistake for Jim to start beating himself up for having an issue with sexual attraction with children when he is reviewing a positive change in dealing with this community safety event.

Instead, Jim and all of us should celebrate those times we have met a community safety challenge in a positive way. This is only to be done once the challenge is completely over, you have met it in a positive way, and you are now completely out of harms way.

The way that you choose to celebrate is a very individualized expression and should not involve anything that others may find offensive. For example, Jim may have added an ice cream cone to his lunch order at the drive through window of the second restaurant. Whatever you choose to do as your celebration, make it brief and enjoyable, without any harm to others, as a way to mark this progress for yourself.

Now add positive modeling, spending time with your mentor, and learning from the experience of others to your toolkit. If you have been reading for a while then stand up and stretch, take a few deep breaths, do a little jig, or otherwise celebrate briefly.

Does it feel like your toolkit is growing? Maybe it is a little heavier. I think we can fit a lot more in there. Let's move on.

As stated earlier, *Choosing Healthy Sexual Boundaries* is not a therapy group. And it is not really an educational class. But group members do, in fact, learn from the group. Sometimes we call this process "Didactic Guidance." We have collected a number of behavior-change techniques and strategies over the years; some of them come from our own journey through treatment and change, while others have been gathered from group participants. They all work. We offer them to the group as suggested practical approaches for staying within boundaries and safe in the community.

CHANGING A SETTING in which unwanted behavior has occurred frequently in the past is simple and practical. Often, we get used to acting-out exclusively in one place. For example, watching pornography late at night in a den or study. Perhaps we feel safe there. We may feel isolated, secretive and unobserved. This is somewhere where we will not be "caught." The presumed safety of these settings helps us give ourselves permission to act inappropriately or illegally. In this case, moving the computer into a common area of the home would be a solid example of "changing the setting."

BREAKING A CHAIN OR CYCLE can help interrupt undesired behavior early enough to maintain good boundaries. This tool is most often useful for men who have participated in a treatment program that required understanding of the components of a personal cycle or chain that leads to unacceptable behavior. These strategies usually remain within the purview of therapy, but once the links are understood and defined, strategies for disrupting the cycle can be formulated and practiced.

REPLACING OR DISPLACING UNDESIRED BEHAVIOR with positive, healthy alternatives is often effective when boundary issues are associated with anxiety, anger, loneliness or boredom. Meditation, relaxation, hobbies or exercise can be incorporated into daily life to help deal with these emotional obstacles. For instance, drinking as a result of boredom, anxiety, sadness or loneliness can be replaced, at least temporarily, by a healthy activity such as walking the dog, or working on your Oil Paint-by-Number kit. You don't have to chose drinking or drugging. This strategy works best if you have a collection or pool of replacement activities from which to choose, and each group member is encouraged to discover or rediscover displacement or replacement pastimes, projects, tasks or undertakings to use appropriately.

FORCED QUIT can be used as a last resort during a difficult challenge. Forced quits occur with computer use when all alternatives to escaping a frozen page have failed. Also known as SHUT IT OUT, STOP-THOUGHT and PUSHING AWAY, during forced quit we convince ourselves that the urge or temptation simply cannot be acted upon at that time. It gets us to safe, functional place.

HAVING A PLAN. When men known that they will be facing a challenging situation, it is always helpful to form an action plan. Perhaps we are seeing old drinking friends in a social (drinking) situation. Maybe visiting a location can be a trigger for acting out. Social anxiety may be a source for concern about a family reunion or a birthday party. Discussing the situation with the group, mapping out a plan using your toolkit, perhaps even rehearsing it with the group, can help assure a healthy and safe outcome to the event.

BOREDOM. An old saying goes, "An idle mind is the devil's playground." With a few word substitutions, we have, "A bored guy's mind is fertile and dangerous ground for his 'Beast' ... or 'Toad'... or perhaps, his 'Addictive Voice.'" However you choose to label or identify your own addiction or "acting-out" behavior, boredom is a primary and constant source of its nourishment. If you have ever attended a substance-abuse support group, then you have heard the ever-present lament, "I relapsed because I was just so bored." Boredom and all forms of addiction and sexual misbehavior are a combustible mix. Boredom can lead to your porn addiction, and then keep you in its grip and control.

So what is boredom? There are lots of definitions, from the anecdotal to the clinical. Wikipedia says it "...is an emotional state experienced when you are left without anything in particular to do, and not interested in your surroundings." A more clinical definition comes from C.D. Fisher. "...an unpleasant, transient state in which the individual feels a pervasive lack of interest, and difficulty concentrating on the current activity." There actually seem to be three types of boredom: times when we are prevented from doing what we want to do, when we are forced to do what we don't want to do, and when we just seem to be unable, for no good reason, to do anything at all. The first two sound suspiciously like being at work. But the third one is of great concern to those of us with poor boundaries. This is the boredom your beast loves most.

For the addicted, boredom often occurs when the addictive behavior is terminated or moderated. What is done to fill the time previously filled with misbehavior? A note here: not everyone with boundary issues is addicted, but every one with an addiction has serious, concomitant boundary problems. So what do we do with this free time? Time we discover after making new boundary choices? How do we overcome boredom?

Lots of folks have lots of strategies for defeating boredom. Google "Boredom" and see for yourself. Some suggestions: try volunteering, writing, cooking, metal detecting or horseback riding. Learn to repair things, watch movies, read more books, build an aquarium or two. Exercise, then paint by numbers. Learn chess, checkers or poker. Make long lists; write some letters. Be social... bored people tend to be boring themselves... don't be that guy. Learn a new skill.

If times of boredom and inactivity are dangerous and risky, fill them up with healthy, safe activities. This is your responsibility. Own it. Do it. Guys sometimes say to us, "I don't really like any of these suggestions. I don't have any interests." Well that doesn't work. Find things that you do like, and then do them. This is not the job of your support group... it is on you.

In Conclusion:
Honor Lost, Honor Regained

A word about honor. Honor earned, lost, regained. Honor has many definitions; many synonyms. Integrity, clear sense of ethical values, respect, character, high moral standards, courage, esteem, honesty, and a strong feel of personal responsibility are a few. "Honor" like its cousin "trust," is hard won, easily lost, and once lost, difficult to regain. It is a fragile thing. Honor can be lost with one act, but more often we lose our honor after a series of poor choices related to ineffective boundaries. Many who have offended suffered loss of honor as a significant consequence. We grieve that loss and wish deeply for its return. Men who attend *Choosing Healthy Sexual Boundaries* often mourn this loss. But honor can be regained, re-earned, reclaimed, just as the "selfs": confidence, esteem, value, respect and image can be re-won. It takes time and great effort, persistence and patience. Choose to behave with integrity, responsibility, trustworthiness, ethics, and high moral values. Be honest with others and with yourself. Project Pathfinder teaches the concept of the Positive Self. Learn to make informed choices, practice goodness in your life, maintain "emotional awareness." Choose to meet your needs in ways that do not harm others. Decide to be the Hero of the rest of your life's story. (You get to write it, you know. Or at least a major part of it.)

This will take time and infinite patience. Others will decide for themselves when they feel you are worthy of honor. You cannot force it, expect it or feel entitled to it from others. Some may learn to see you as an honorable man; others will not. But whatever the outcome, you can take pride in your efforts to return to, or become, a man of honor. It can be done. We have seen it happen many times. You can do it too. Perhaps a support group like *Choosing Healthy Sexual Boundaries* could help you.

Final Note on the Essence of Support Groups...

Men sometimes come to us after a period of absence from the group. They tell us that they skipped because they did not have much to say. Or that things are going good, and that they didn't feel a need to come to the group for a while. These statements miss the essence of being a good group member. A support group should not be "crisis intervention" only. Support groups are a two-way street. You get support; you give support. When you accept the support of a group, you accept responsibility to return support. If you are feeling good, if you have little check-in, there is still much positive you can accomplish by attending your group. Nothing to say? Then listen. By listening to others, by attending to their thoughts and feelings and ideas, you are providing support and validation. Support groups are not just about you. They are about the group and its members. There are always men within a support group who have spent much of their lives with feelings that have not been acknowledged or validated. Thoughtless or cruel parents, insensitive teachers, and self-absorbed, egocentric friends have disregarded, ignored and minimized their feelings throughout their lives. This is an opportunity to give to the group, and to individuals within your group. Do it. The group will be there when you do need it.

And Finally... Pulling it Together

Peer-facilitated, community-based support groups play an important part in the continuum of mental health care. The men and women who attend these groups are often marginalized, have little or limited health care insurance and often have no, or exhausted, mental health benefits. Although volunteer-based groups may exist at the "bottom" of the health care pyramid, they do provide a safe, comfortable, confidential, inexpensive or free venue in which to discuss important personal issues. While support groups do not provide therapy, they are often therapeutic in nature and function.

Choosing Healthy Sexual Boundaries: The Handbook resulted from such a support group. We have discussed various aspects of the group's purpose and function. We hope that you have learned something about the basics of boundaries; identifying, choosing and maintaining them, and that you have gained knowledge about how to determine strong from weak or poorly chosen boundaries. And of course, we hope that this handbook will help you in your quest for better choices and stronger, safer boundaries. Good luck in your journey.

References

Behavior, Wikipedia (2014)
http://en.wikipedia.org/wiki/Behavior

Boredom, Wikipedia (2014)
http://en.wikipedia.org/wiki/Boredom

Ellis, Albert, Interview by Robert Epstein, published in *Psychology Today* (2001)
http://www.psychologytoday.com/articles/200101/the-prince-reason

Fisher, Cynthia D., *"Boredom at work: a neglected concept"* (1991). School of Business Discussion Papers. Paper 19.
http://epublications.bond.edu.au/discussion_papers/19

Frost, Robert, *Mending Wall*, published in *North of Boston* poetry collection (1917)
Henry Holt And Company,
http://www.gutenberg.org/ebooks/3026

Fox, Vincent, *Self-Worth – What it is and is not.* (1989)
http://www.smartrecovery.org/resources/library/Articles_and_Essays/Self-Acceptance/usa.htm

Hare, Robert, *Hare Psychopathy Checklist – Revised (PCL-R)*, (1991) http://www.hare.org
http://en.wikipedia.org/wiki/Hare_Psychopathy_Checklist

Peele, Stanton, *Love and Addiction* (1975), *The Meaning of Addiction* (1985/1998), *The Truth about Addiction and Recovery* (with Archie Brodsky and Mary Arnold, 1991), *Resisting 12-Step Coercion* (with Charles Bufe and Archie Brodsky, 2001), *7 Tools to Beat Addiction* (2004), and *Recover! Stop Thinking Like an Addict* (with Ilse Thompson, 2014) http://en.wikipedia.org/wiki/Stanton_Peele

Resources

MNATSA (Minnesota Association for the Treatment of Sex Abusers), http://www.mnatsa.org

Minnesota Mankind Project, P.O. Box 141018, Minneapolis, MN 55414
http://minnesota.mkp.org

Project Pathfinder, 1821 University Ave W, St Paul, MN 55104
http://www.projectpathfinder.org

RATIONAL Recovery, PO Box 800, Lotus CA 95651
https://www.rational.org

Ron Hering Award, Mankind Project, info@mkp.org
http://mankindproject.org/missions

Sex Addicts Anonymous, ISO of SAA, PO Box 70949, Houston, TX 77270
https://saa-recovery.org

Sexaholics Anonymous, PO Box 3565, Brentwood, TN 37024
http://www.sa.org

SMART Recovery, 7304 Mentor Avenue, Suite F, Mentor, OH 44060
http://www.smartrecovery.org

Twin Cities Men's Center, 3249 Hennepin Avenue South, Suite 55, Minneapolis, MN 55408, http://www.tcmc.org

Veteran's Administration, 1-877-222-VETS (8387)
http://www.mentalhealth.va.gov/index.asp

48

CPSIA information can be obtained
at www.ICGtesting.com
Printed in the USA
LVHW09s2316170918
590493LV00001B/25/P

9 781456 621933

In an arena of social turbulence, social stigma, fear and anger, two me
quietly set about changing the way sex offenders view themselves...

*...This makes it possible for primary prevention to take place by the people who possess th
greatest insight. Tommy and Bobby began something historic with the founding of their H
Boundaries group. This book is equally historic. "Good judgment comes from experience;
experience comes from bad judgment," is the old saying. Most sexual abuse is committed e
everyday people who make incredibly bad choices. How do we make a change? Follow the
advice in this book.*

Warren Maas
Executive Director, Project Pathfinder, Inc.

---

*This book is the culmination of 10 years of patient listening and unconditional acceptance
among men sitting in a trusted circle. It provides accessible tips and lifelines for those who
to establish and maintain healthy sexuality. It models compassion, support and accountab
essential in an effective social response to sexual abusers. This book, comprised of others'
experiences, provides hope and meaningful tools to prevent future sexual harm. We owe or
gratitude to the authors; two wise humble and honorable men who recognize and respect th
human potential for transformation.*

Jannine Hébert
Executive Clinical Director
Minnesota Sex Offender Program

---

*Over the last 10 years, Bobby and Tommy have helped men improve their lives through th
Healthy Sexual Boundaries support group at the Twin Cities Men's Center. In so doing,
have also helped improve the lives of countless family, friends and community members. A
outgrowth of that group, this handbook addresses an intimidating subject in an easy to re
and approachable way, and offers clear strategies for identifying and choosing healthy
boundaries. It will undoubtedly help many more men everywhere.*

Joe Szurszewski
Board Chair, Twin Cities Men's Center

Choosing Healthy Sexual Boundaries: The Handbook
© 2014 Tommy Jones and Bobby Schauerhamer
Cover and layout by Bill Dobbs, www.animuse.com
Printed by eBookIt.com, www.eBookIt.com

ISBN 978-1-4566-

USA $7.99

9 781456 621933

Casanova in Venice

A RAUNCHY RHYME

Kildare Dobbs